IRELAND TRAVEL A
BOOK AND JOURNAL

This book belongs to:

_____

First published in 2019 by Family A Go Go

Text and Illustration copyright © 2019 Family A Go Go

Written and Illustrated by: Lauren Kotwal

www.familyagogobooks.com

MARK WHERE YOU TRAVELED AND WHAT YOU SAW!

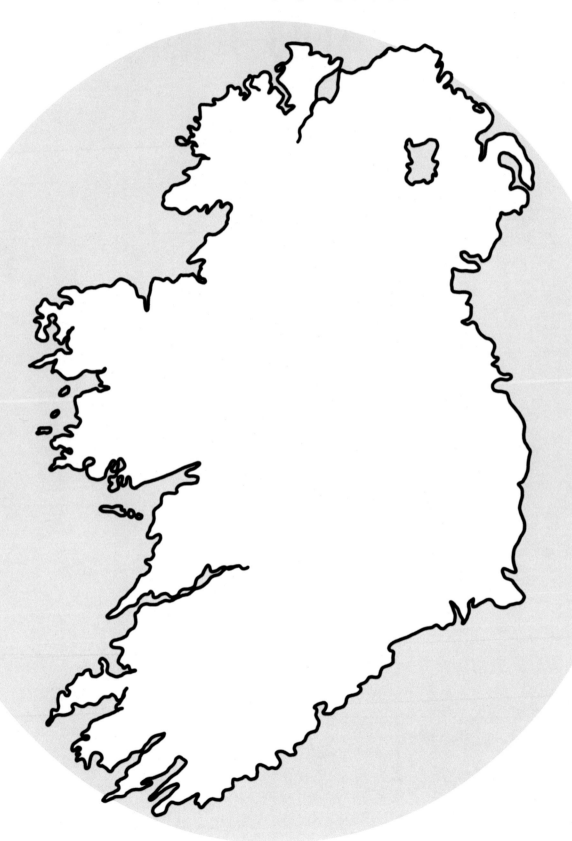

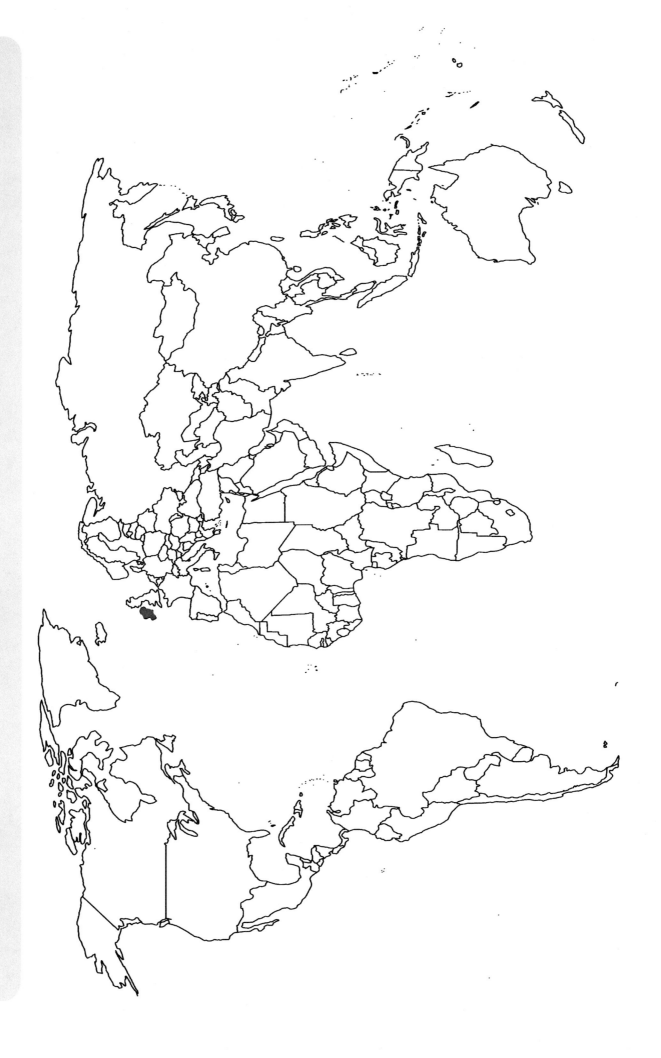

FIND THE MATCHING SHAMROCKS!

BINGO!

Shamrock	Fiddle	Pub	Fox
Rabbit	Fairy door	Castle	Gargoyle
Beach	Stone circle	Bog	Tea
Shepards pie	Guinness van	Ruins	Sheep

HISTORY

People first settled in Ireland around 6000 BC. Around 700 BC the Celts came from central Europe to the island. They brought their technologically advanced culture and lived here for nearly 2,000 years.

Vikings began raids into Ireland in the 9th century AD. They established settlements that later became some of the County's main cities, including Dublin. The Vikings and Celts fought for 200 years. Eventually, the people of Ireland divided into many smaller kingdoms.

In 1170, the English invaded the island and made it an English territory. There were frequent fighting between the Irish and the English. By the 1820s, England had made many laws that were unfair to Catholics living in Ireland. Many of the laws were overturned, but Ireland still wanted freedom. In 1922 the Irish Free State was created within the British Empire.

In 1948, most of Ireland became an independent country, while the six (mainly Protestant) counties in the northeast remained a British territory. There was lots of fighting between the two sides after this split (often referred to as "the trouble"). Today there is peace between north Ireland and the Republic of Ireland.

MYTHICAL FIGURES

Irish myths and legends are an important part of the history of Ireland. These myths and legends have endured and have shaped Irish culture.

FAERIES

In Irish mythology, faerie folk (or asos si) are supernatural beings or nature spirits, and are usually invisible and much smaller than humans. They are said to live in underground faerie mounds, across the western sea, or in an invisible world that coexists with the world of humans. There are many different types of faeries, and some can be helpful to humans, and some can be dangerous or mean if you offend them.

"Faerie Faith" are beliefs and practices carried out by those who want to keep on the good side of faeries. People who believe often follow old customs of leaving milk and food for the faeries.

Today, there are faerie trails all over Ireland that you can explore. Each faerie trail is different, but they all usually have a trail for you to explore and find all the faerie doors and houses.

THE SHAMROCK

The National Flower is the shamrock. The shamrock has come to represent the "luck of the Irish."

LEPRECHAUNS

Leprechauns are one type of faerie folk and are said to be found in faerie forts. They are usually thought of as small elf-like figures wearing emerald green clothes and usually sporting a beard and smoking a pipe. According to legend, if you manage to capture one of these mischievous creatures, he will be forced to hand over his stash of gold. Some legends say that their pots of gold are also hidden at the end of a rainbow.

WILL-O'-THE-WISPS

Will-o'-the-wisps are lights that are seen over boggy areas by travelers at night in Ireland and Britain. There are many different legends about these lights...sometimes they are said to lead people astray. Sometimes they help guide people to what they seek. If you ever see these lights, it might be best to stay away.

IRISH DIALECT

The people in Ireland mostly speak English as their primary language. The Gaelic language is also spoken - mostly spoken in the west side of the country. Here are some of the Irish or Gaelic words and phrases you may hear when visiting Ireland. Practice saying them before you go!

"Fáilte" (pronounced like "fall-sha") - welcome
Ath cliath (pronounced "ah cli-a") - Another name for Dublin and is on road signs
An Lár - City center
Seirbhís (pronounced service) - In service. Seen on buses
As seirbhís - "out of service"
The toilets/the jacks - bathroom
Mná - woman
Fir - man
Quare (pronounced "queer") - very
The press - cupboard

Wrecked - very tired
The guards/Garda - police
Diesel/petrol - gas
The boot - trunk of the car
Chips - french fries
Jumper - sweater
The messages - groceries
Siáinte (pronounced slaan-sha) - Cheers!
Beyont - Any place that is beyond the place you are in at the moment
"Sure look it" - An acceptable response to any question
"Wet the tea" - put boiling water on tea bags

MONEY

There are two countries on the island, and they each use a different currency. The Republic of Ireland is part of the European Union and uses the Euro. Northern Ireland uses the Pound Sterling.

Republic of Ireland Euros

Northern Ireland Pound Sterling

IRISH FOOD

Many Irish dishes feature potatoes as the main ingredient. Traditional meals are very hearty foods that are designed to fill you up. Foods like this are very important after a hard day's work and cold wet weather. The following are some of the foods you might find on your travels.

Irish Stews
Stews are traditionally made with lamb or beef

Blaa
A type of bread that may only be called "blaa" if it is made in County Waterford. Usually only made/sold on Saturday mornings

Soda bread
A very popular bread that is usually eaten with a main meal

Boxty
A type of potato pancake

Colcannon
Mash potatoes made with milk, butter, and scallions

Shepherd's pie
A meat pie made with a crust or topping of mashed potatoes

Bacon and Cabbage
Cooked cabbage with bacon, potatoes, and gravy

Full Irish
Traditional breakfast that comes with meat, eggs, pudding, tomatoes, and bread

Circle the foods you tried!

MAKE YOUR OWN SODA BREAD

RECIPE

4 cups all purpose flour
4 Tbs white sugar
1 Tsp baking soda
1 Tbs baking powder
½ Tsp salt

½ cup butter, softened
1 cup buttermilk
1 egg
¼ cup butter and ¼ cup buttermilk for brushing

Preheat oven to 375 degrees F (190 degrees C). Lightly grease a large baking sheet.

In a large bowl, mix together flour, sugar, baking soda, baking powder, salt and margarine. Stir in 1 cup of buttermilk and egg. Turn dough out onto a lightly floured surface and knead slightly. Form dough into a round and place on prepared baking sheet. In a small bowl, combine melted butter with 1/4 cup buttermilk; brush loaf with this mixture. Use a sharp knife to cut an 'X' into the top of the loaf.

Bake in preheated oven until a toothpick inserted into the center of the loaf comes out clean, 45 to 50 minutes. Check for doneness after 30 minutes. You may continue to brush the loaf with the butter mixture while it bakes.

What do you think of the soda bread you made?

How does soda bread taste in Ireland?

SPORTS

Hurling

Hurling is one of the most popular sports in Ireland. It has ancient Gaelic origins. The object of the game is for players to use a wooden (ash) stick called a "hurley" to hit a small ball between goal posts. They get one point for going over the goal's cross bar, or three points for going under. Players can use their hands, feet, and stick to move the ball up and down the field.

Gaelic Football

While sharing a similar name, Gaelic football is quite different than the football played around the world. In this game, players can carry, bounce, kick, or hand-pass the ball. In the game, two types of scores are possible: points and goals. A point is awarded for kicking or hand-passing the ball over the crossbar. A goal is awarded for kicking the ball under the crossbar into the net (this one is worth more points!)

Rugby

Rugby is a very rough sport. American football actually came from rugby. There are two different leagues that have their owns rules (League and Union).

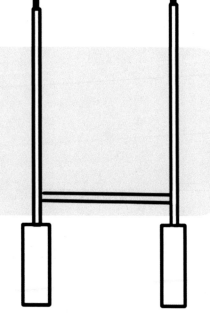

CASTLES

There are about 3,000 castles spread all across Ireland. The most impressive castles were built around the late 1100s. Today, many castles are in ruins, but others have been preserved. You can visit many of these, and you can even spend the night in some of them! Below are some of the interesting castles you can visit in Ireland:

Ashford Castle

Ashford Castle was built in 1228 by a member of the Guinness family, and it looks like it is straight out of a fairy tale. There are many towers and turrets, and it is located on lush green grounds next to a lake. It is now a luxury hotel with a falconry.

Blarney Castle

Blarney Castle is one of Ireland's biggest tourist attractions because of the Blarney Stone. According to stories, kissing the stone gives the kisser the "gift of gab." Today people line up to hang their heads over the edge of the castle wall to kiss the stone.

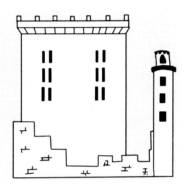

The Rock of Cashel

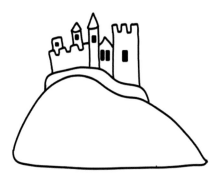

The Rock of Cashel is one of the most visited heritage sites in Ireland because it has it all! The walled complex contains a castle, cathedral, and chapel. It is also a 5 minute walk from the town of Cashel, which has a replica folk village that depicts early country life in Ireland. The grounds are open year-round with free admission on the first Wednesday of every month.

Ballynahinch Castle

Ballynahinch Castle was once the home of a pirate queen! Grace O'Malley would frequently stop ships sailing off the coast and take part of their cargo. Today, you can stay at the castle, go salmon fishing, bike riding, or hike in the surrounding trails.

IRISH DANCING AND MUSIC

MUSIC

It is said that traditional Irish music embodies the spirit of the Irish people. Traditional Irish music is upbeat and it is very easy to join in by clapping your hands or dancing a jig. There are two types of traditional music that you might hear when in Ireland:

Seisún (pronounced she-shoon) is an informal gathering of musicians. Usually it will kick off with a guitar, and then fiddlers, flutists, banjos, and drums will join in. People clap along with the beat as dancers twirl and skip around. Don't be afraid to join in! No one minds if you don't know the steps! You can find a pub seisún in nearly every village, town and city on the island.

Céilí (pronounced kay-lee) is a social gathering featuring Irish music and dance, and its the focus is on dancing. Locals will demand that you join in. There will be different styles of dance and music depending on which part of the country you are in.

DANCE

Irish dancing is a group of traditional dance forms and can be done alone or in groups. Step dancing is a form of solo dancing and involves a stiff upper body and intricate footwork. Ceili dance is performed in groups of two to sixteen people. The footwork is simple and the formations made with the dancers is the most important part.

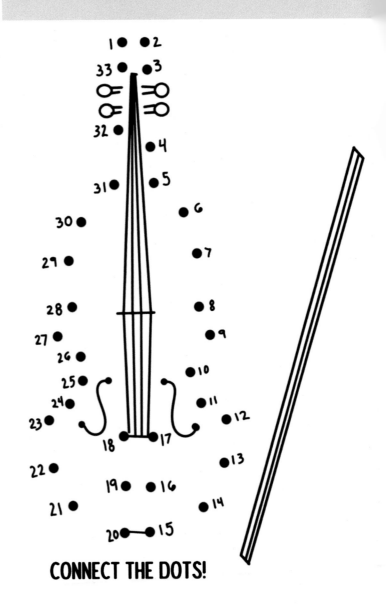

CONNECT THE DOTS!

PEAT BOGS

The peat bog is one of the most common parts of the Irish landscape that you will see if you leave Dublin. Bogs cover more than 1/6th of the island. Peat bogs are a type of wetland that are made up of dead and decaying vegetation. They are home to a unique ecosystem, with dozens of plants and animals that are perfectly adapted to life in the bog and are found nowhere else. Bogs are spongy and often impossible to move through.

Bogs have long been important to the Irish people. The bog material has been used as a source of fuel for hundreds of years. They are also very important culturally because bogs are very good at preserving artifacts that have fallen into the bogs over the centuries (even human bodies!). These items are well preserved because the bogs contain a type of moss that has special preservatives. After the moss dies, it decays very slowly, as does anything that falls into the bogs. These objects have allowed us to learn a lot about the ways people lived hundreds and thousands of years ago.

STRANGE THINGS FOUND IN PEAT BOGS

 More than 270 kegs of "bog butter." It is sometimes butter, and sometimes meat. The bogs likely acted as an ancient refrigerator to preserve the food.

Preserved bodies

Swords and ornaments

Old books. One book, more than 1,000 years old was found, and you could still read the writing!

DRAW SOME THINGS YOU COULD FIND IN A BOG

ANIMALS OF IRELAND

There are only 26 land mammals, one lizard, and three amphibian species native to Ireland. When Ireland was connected to the mainland, some species like wild boars, lynx, and brown bears, managed to make it across—as did a single reptile: the common lizard. But when the sea levels began to rise after the ice age, the area was cut off from the mainland. Any animal that didn't make it over before Ireland was cut off missed their chance.

Some species, such as the red fox, European hedgehog, stoat, otter, pygmy shrew, and badger are frequently seen around the island. However, the Irish hare, red deer, and pine marten are less common and generally seen only in certain national parks and nature preserves around the island.

There are no wild snakes in Ireland! Legend says that St. Patrick used his power to drive all of the snakes into the sea. But in truth, there were never any snakes in Ireland because they never made it over when the island was connected to The mainland.

DRAW YOUR FAVORITE ANIMAL SIGHTING

COLOR THE NATIONAL BIRD OF IRELAND

THE NORTHERN LAPWING

NORTHERN IRELAND — BELFAST

Northern Ireland is the smallest of the four parts of the United Kingdom. This area is sometimes called Ulster because it includes six of the nine counties that made up the ancient kingdom of Ulster. The landscape of Northern Ireland consists of rolling hills surrounded by low mountains.

The capital city of Northern Ireland is Belfast. This area was once dangerous when there was fighting between Northern Ireland and the Republic of Ireland, but Belfast is now one of the safest cities in the United Kingdom.

There are lots of fun places to visit in Belfast! Here are a few ideas to get you started:

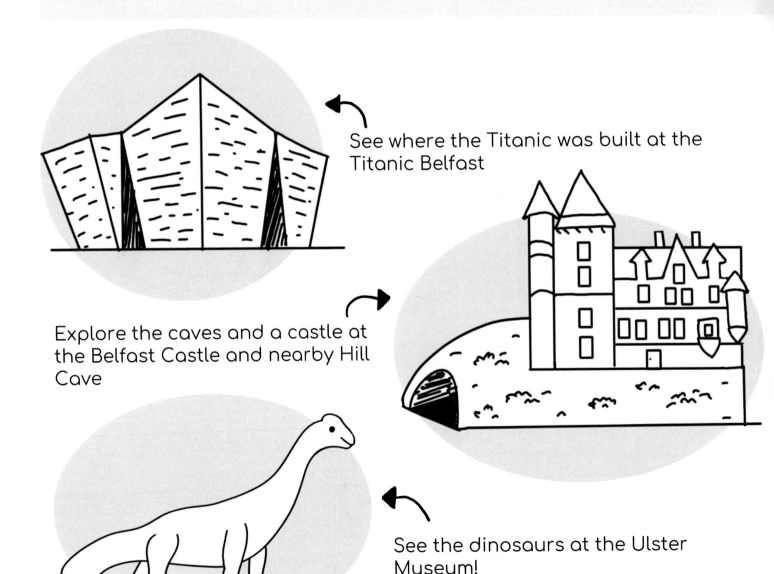

See where the Titanic was built at the Titanic Belfast

Explore the caves and a castle at the Belfast Castle and nearby Hill Cave

See the dinosaurs at the Ulster Museum!

THE GIANTS CAUSEWAY

The northern part of the Northern Ireland coast is made up of thousands of basalt rock columns. The best place to see this rock formation is at the Giant's Causeway.

Legend says that a giant called Finn McCool built a path of rocks across the sea to Scotland so that he could battle a rival giant. The truth is *almost* as interesting...the columns were created by a super-volcanic eruptions over 60 million years ago.

DRAW A PICTURE OF GIANTS WALKING ON THE GIANT'S CAUSEWAY

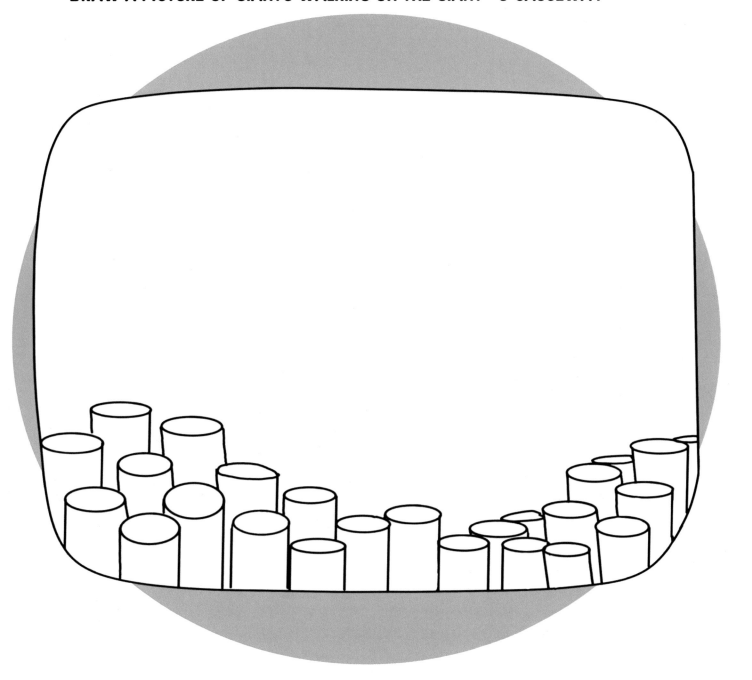

DUBLIN

Dublin is the capital of the Republic of Ireland, and has countless things to do and see, depending on your interests and the weather. Here are a few ideas!

St. Stephen's Green
This a beautiful green park in the center of Dublin that was opened to the public in 1880. Visit the lake, waterfalls, sculptures, and playground.

National Gallery of Ireland
The museum opened in 1864 with a focus on Irish art, but also includes other European art. Admission is free!

Dublin is an Old Irish Gaelic phrase that translates to "Black Pool" due to the dark lake that was once there

Trinity College
The college was founded by Queen Elizabeth I in 1592 and is Ireland's oldest surviving university. There is a lot for visitors to see here, including the Book of Kells Exhibition in the Old Library building, the science gallery, and the zoological museum.

St Annes Park
Dublin's second largest public park is beautiful with wonderful coastal views. The estate was assembled by members of the Guinness family. The park features many follies, a river, duck pond, and walled garden. Keep your eyes peeled for badgers, hedgehogs, rabbits, foxes, squirrels, and mice.

Dublinia
A living history museum that focuses on viking and medieval history. It is located in part of Dublin's Christ Church Cathedral. It features period-houses, buildings, street scenes, and actors dressed up as vikings.

The Ark
A space in the center of Dublin's Temple Bar district where children (ages 2-12) can explore theatre, music, literature, art, film, dance and watch performances.

Nearby Areas
Hop on the commuter train and visit some of these smaller towns.
- To the south: Dún Laoghaire, Killiney, and Bray,
- To the north: Howth

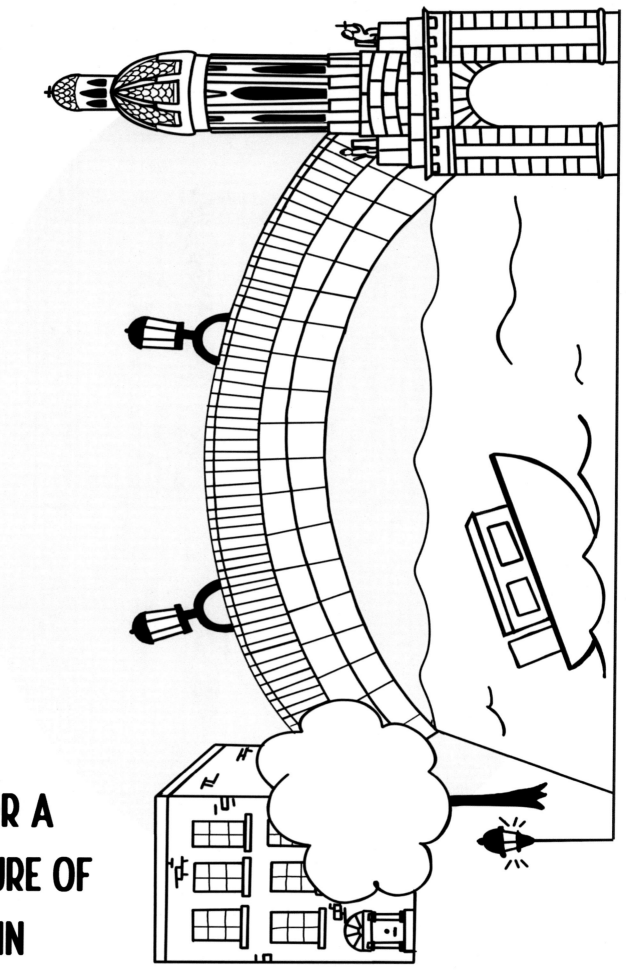

COLOR A
PICTURE OF
DUBLIN

BOOK OF KELLS

The Book of Kells is an illuminated manuscript containing the four Gospels of the New Testament. It was created in a monastery in either Britain or Ireland and is believed to have been created around 800 AD. You can see one page per day at the Old Library building at Trinity College.

COUNTY WICKLOW

South of Dublin you will find County Wicklow, which is known as the Garden of Ireland. This area has something for everyone with beautiful coastlines, woodlands, and mountains (the second highest peak in Ireland can be found here). It is also the home to Wicklow Way, which is the country's most popular walking trail. It will take you along old bog roads, forest trails, and disused military supply lines. Be sure to stop at the Glendalough Monastic ruins, explore the large and impressive Powerscourt House and nearby waterfall, hike or kayak around Lough Dan, have a picnic around Lough Tay (aka Guinness Lake), and pause at the Sally Gap for amazing views of the surrounding bogs and Wicklow Mountains. Along the coast, you can stop in the charming town of Bray and visit SEA LIFE Bray to see a variety of sea life, see farm animals on the peaceful Glenroe Farm, or relax on a big stretch of beach and sand dunes at Brittas Bay.

FIND YOUR WAY TO THE CENTER OF THE HEDGE MAZE!

COUNTY CORK

County Cork is on the southern part of the island. This area has some of the most famous sites in Ireland. Here you will find Blarney Castle and will have the chance to hang upside down and kiss the famous Blarney Stone. The Beara Peninsula is an amazing area to hike and take pictures. Take ferries to some of the islands that dot the coastline where you can find ruins, views, and places to swim. And Ballydehob in West Cork has several prehistoric Celtic standing stones to explore.

DESIGN A FAIRY DOOR!

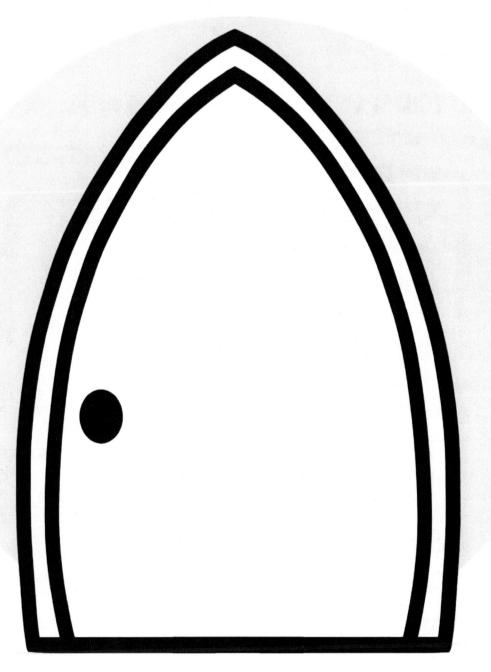

COUNTY KERRY

One of the most popular attractions in County Kerry is the Ring of Kerry. It is a circular tourist route with many interesting sights along the way. Stop at the Killarney National Park to see beautiful views, hike, or even take a pony ride. Other places to explore are the Crag Cave, Torq Waterfall, Gap of Dunloe, and the Blue Flag Beaches. You can also stop in the small port town of Dingle to see an unusual celebrity - Fungie the Dingle dolphin! This dolphin has been guiding fishing boats to and from the Dingle Harbor for years. You can even take a boat trip just to say hello.

DRAW SOME THINGS YOU SAW ALONG THE RING OF KERRY!

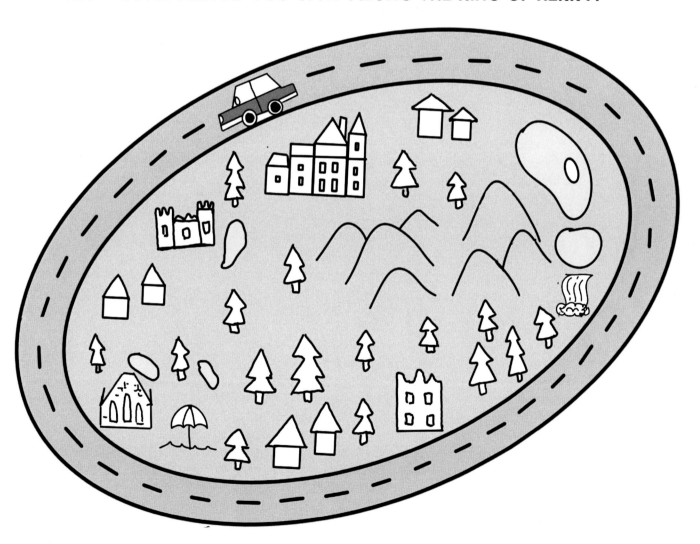

COUNTY CLARE

County Clare is in western Ireland and has both rolling countryside and craggy Atlantic coastline. One of the best things to do here is see the Cliffs of Moher. Here the cliffs rise 702 feet about the ocean. O'brien's Tower is on top of the cliffs and offers dramatic views of the surrounding cliffs and ocean.

Another fun area to explore is the Burren. This is a unique rocky wilderness area that contains Stone Age monuments and ancient churches. Here you can also find the longest cave system in Ireland.

DRAW YOURSELF ON THE CLIFFS OF MOHER

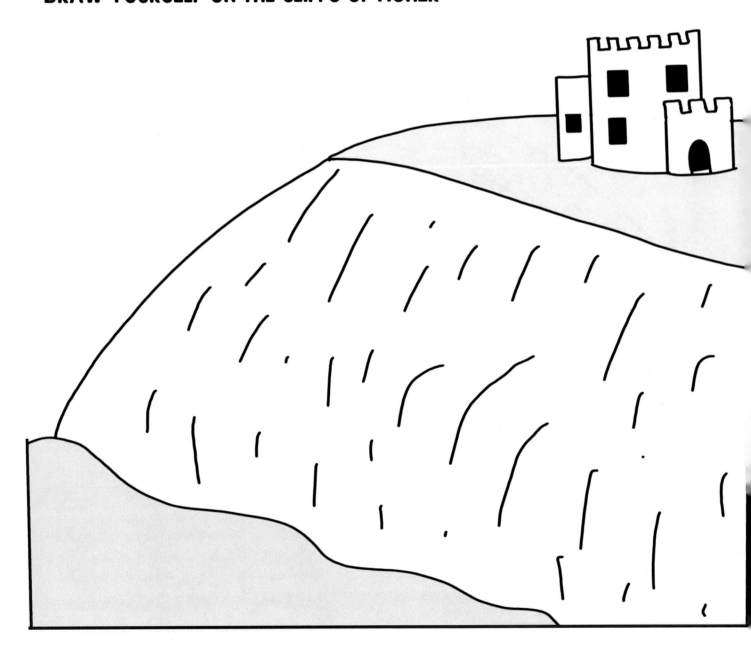

COUNTY GALWAY

County Galway is also along the western portion of the island, and it is known for its natural beauty. Drive along Sky Road to see some of the best views of the coast in the county. Connemara National Park includes scenic mountains, bogs, heaths, grasslands, and woodlands. There are three main walking routes throughout the park and each offers different scenery and wildlife all along the way. If you are interested in castles, you can visit Dunguaire Castle or Kylemore Abbey. Kylemore Abbey is a beautiful building set on the edge of a lake, and there are places all around to play and explore.

DRAW PEOPLE AND THINGS IN THE CASTLE WINDOWS

COLOR A PICTURE OF THE MOUNTAIN HARE
- A NATIONAL ANIMAL OF IRELAND

COLOR IN THE FAERIES

DRAW IN SOME WINGS, EYES, AND FEATHER PATTERNS!

DRAW A PICTURE OF WHAT YOU DID TODAY

DRAW A PICTURE OF WHAT YOU DID TODAY

DRAW A PICTURE OF WHAT YOU DID TODAY

DRAW A PICTURE OF WHAT YOU DID TODAY

DRAW A PICTURE OF WHAT YOU DID TODAY

DRAW A PICTURE OF WHAT YOU DID TODAY

DRAW A PICTURE OF HOW YOU TRAVELED HERE

WHAT WAS THE BEST PLACE YOU STAYED?

WHAT WAS THE BEST THING YOU ATE?

WHAT WAS THE BEST THING YOU DID?

Doodle Page!

Doodle Page!

Doodle Page!

Made in the USA
Monee, IL
13 December 2022

21507017R00026